The Spider and the Caterpillar

Written by
Anthony Patrick Heeter

Illustrated by
Ananta Mohanta

Copyright

This is a work of fiction. Names, characters, places, and incidents either are the product of the author's imagination or are used fictitiously. Any resemblance to actual persons, living or dead, events, or locations is entirely coincidental.

First print edition November 2023

Illustrations by: Ananta Mohanta
Book Design by: Joyce Licorish
Published by: DreamEmpire Publishing

ISBN 9798865959106 (paperback) - AMAZON
ISBN979-8-8689-5822-9 (hardcover) - INGRAM

www.AnthonyPatrickHeeter.com

Dedication

First and foremost, I take great delight in thanking everyone who has believed in and encouraged me along this path of self-discovery and art. I'd love to thank everyone who has seen my love, light, and greatness and never let me forget that I am created for more than I could have imagined. Every one of you has and always will have, a space in my existence. All of you have been a light to my footsteps, a shoulder to lean on, an ear to hear my voice, providers of words of wisdom, and teachers of illumination. I have so much gratitude for you all and pray that as you step into your destiny, you are blessed with people in your lives who bless you as you have blessed me.

I want to extend love and gratitude to my daughter, Lily. Your boundless love has taught me that life isn't about perfection but consistent love. I want to thank Vincent Minor; you are my friend and, even more, my brother. Your hard truths have made me see myself for who I am and have opened my eyes to my greatest potential. I am beyond thankful for your words of encouragement and love.

I want to thank you, Joyce, and Dreamempire, for your belief in my artistic greatness and for adding me to a group of esteemed artists such as yourselves. You are a bright light and have been blessed with a spirit to discover and uplift greatness.

I thank you, my Samwise Gamgee, Ryan Triddy. Your brotherly love, encouragement, and confirmations have been pivotal to my self-discovery. You are the most special of friends, and I honor you with all my heart.

Again, a special thanks to everyone who has encouraged me along this journey. I am honored and humbled and pray that you enjoy this book.
-Anthony Patrick Heeter

There once was a Spider and Caterpillar
that shared their home in a tree.
Every day they would wake,
and each other they would greet.

From late Spring showers
to the early summer breeze,
they would wake up each morning,
wave and would speak.

"Hello Spider, so elegant, so sleek."

"Hello caterpillar, how are you, my sweet?"

"Well, thank you.
Just looking for something to eat."

"Well, come by anytime Caterpillar,
and I'll make you a feast!"

Days flew by as
they would pass
and they'd greet.

Caterpillar would
pipe up each time
that they'd meet.

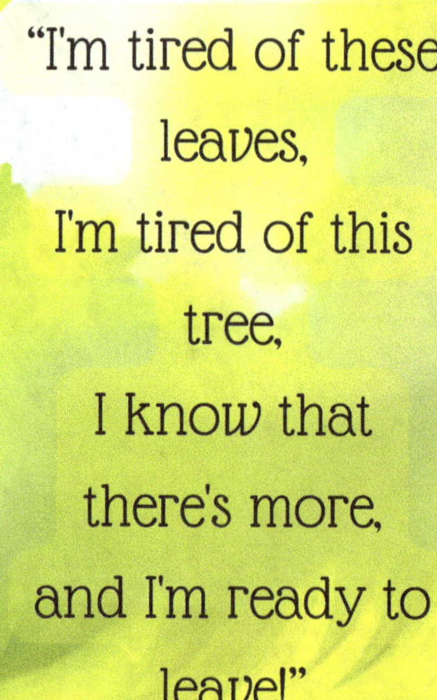

"I'm tired of these
leaves,
I'm tired of this
tree,
I know that
there's more,
and I'm ready to
leave!"

"Tired of leaves? Tired of the tree?
Caterpillar seriously, you're ready to leave?
Where would you go? Oh, don't you know,
a caterpillar is all that you'll ever be?"

"Caterpillar, if you're tired of the tree and all of these leaves, just come on in, and I'll make you a feast."

"Tired of leaves? Tired of the tree?
Caterpillar seriously, you're ready to leave?
Where would you go? Oh, don't you know,
a caterpillar is all that you'll ever be?"

"Caterpillar, if you're tired of the tree and all of these leaves, just come on in, and I'll make you a feast."

"Maybe some other time, Spider, I'm tired and beat. I'll see you tomorrow, tomorrow we'll speak. But mark my words, Spider. One day, I'm going to leave!"

A morning sunrise, beating with summer's heat.
Caterpillar wakes sluggish, slow in his speech,
"Hello, Spider, so elegant, so sleek."
"Hello, Caterpillar, how are we, my sweet?"
"Well, thank you. Just looking for something to eat.
I'm just tired of only eating these same old leaves.
I have made up my mind. I'm packing my things.
It's time to go, I'm ready to leave."

"Caterpillar, you're serious?
You're going to leave?
What about your home?
What about me?
Who will I have each morning to greet?
Caterpillar I ask, if it must be?
Let me cook you a meal,
let me make you a feast."
Mail
welcome

"Caterpillar, you're serious?
You're going to leave?
What about your home?
What about me?
Who will I have each morning to greet?
Caterpillar I ask, if it must be?
Let me cook you a meal,
let me make you a feast."
Mail
Welcome

"If you'll just step
inside,
inside you will see,
my beautiful place
for a beautiful feast."

"Spider, thank you.
You're so elegant, so sleek.
I must be one lucky caterpillar to be invited
to a feast by Spider so sweet."

"Yes, Caterpillar, I truly agree.
We are lucky.
Both lucky indeed.
But first, before a bite,
let's have a drink."

"A drink you say?
No Spider, a toast!
A toast, to the most
wonderful host."

"Yes Caterpillar, and also to the feast. So let's raise up our glass and have us drink!"
GULP!

"Thank you Spider, so
elegant and sleek.
Your sweetness expressed
inside of the drink.

So sorry Spider, I spilled
my drink. So truly spider
I must leave.
Oh my head, oh my feet,
I think I should lie down,
I think I need to sleep.
I'll be going now, but
thanks to you, enjoy
your feast."

"Wait, oh wait Caterpillar, before
you just go.
I feel terrible that you're ill,
and too tired to leave so,
I made a bed for your head,
a place to prop up your feet.
Rest for now, but before you wake,
I'll prepare the feast."

"Oh thank you Spider so elegant, so sleek.
Who would have known a Spider could be so sweet?"

"Thank you for the bed Spider.
Thank you for each sheet.
Thank you for the blankets,
and thank you for how tight you
tucked me in, you're so sweet."

"You're welcome Catapillar,
and is it just me?
You look so delightful,
so delectable, and sweet."

"Rest for now Caterpillar.
Soon it'll be time to eat."

Three days have passed,
with Caterpillar not
making a squirm.
Spider paced impatiently, "I
can't wait to eat this little
worm!"

"Tap, tap, tap, anyone inside?" Spider calls to Caterpillar.
"It's time to come out. I have a surprise!"

Spider can't take it anymore,
She slashes with all her might,
but with each swipe,
she only scratches the side.

Spider is worn and the blade
has grown dull.
Spider says,
"I'm sooo hungry.
But it's like trying to cut
through a brick wall."

"Tap, tap, tap! Anyone inside?"

Spider desperately calls to Caterpillar.

"It's time to come out! I have a surprise."

"One moment, please."
Spider heard Caterpillar's chime.
"I'm coming out! It's time, it's time!"

An explosion ensued,
Spider was knocked back,
shaking the web's morning dew.
Spider in awe says,
"Caterpillar, is that really you?"

"Look at those wings!
You're so different,
so radiant too."

"Spider, There's always been more to me, you just never knew."

"No more a Caterpiller, now let's see what these wings can really do!"

"Spread out my wings.
Fly so smooth."

"Each flutter like
butter through the air
I cut through."

"Now I must leave,
enjoy the feast.
My destiny is New!"